Encyclopedia of Decoding Death. Start.Longago.start How the Brain Calculates Day Of Death with 1000% Accuracy.

David Gomadza

www.twofuture.world

Copyright © 2024 David Gomadza

All rights reserved.

PAPERBACK ISBN: 9798322909422

DEDICATION

To a better future.

CONTENTS

ACKNOWLEDGMENTS

A big thanks to Tomorrow's World Order

START.LONGAGO.START HOW THE BRAIN CALCULATES DEATH WITH ASTONISHING ACCURACY

Start.longago.start
How the body calculates day of death with1000% accuracy.
The body over the years has developed a clever system that predicts with astonishing accuracy the day of death of anyone that means anyone can know when another person is likely to die if we look at how the body does this this is how
The body over the years will record everything from happiness to sadness and will keep track of everything on a daily basis as a general rule the more happy you are the more and longer you live if we look at how the body calculates this this is how the body over years will add an extra year to your life just for being you that means if you do everything it predicts then every year your life will increase by one year but humans don't understand what the body needs for the first time in the history of
mankind I am the only one to be able to talk to the brain
Now if we Ask the brain why this is so this is the reply we look at how he is inside and it's something no one else has that means this man is unique hence his capabilities this format of body configuration is only found in gods and never humans therefore the question is is this [me- David Gomadza] human or something else?
Now let's look at how the body does this The body has a sequence of doing this and this is the first sequence the body identifies the causal effects to death and the hindrance effects to long life and compute an algorithm that it uses to calculate likely death day in doing so it makes sure that it uses everything well in accordance to this day otherwise it will have loads of say protein on day of death
which is known to be inaccurate because in brain circles lack of protein means death it is believed among the brain that lack of protein is death meaning no one with protein is supposed to day
Now if we look at this further we can see that people neglect every advise given by people who study the brain but some of the advise is correct if we look at things that cause death in humans they are all to do with our lifestyles our habits and what we eat or don't eat
Now let's look at what causes death in the first place death is

4

caused by a lot of things from improper eating to overeating if we Ask what needs doing then this need doing humans must speak to their brains as I do then they must listen the brain knows what is good or bad but humans insist on what is bad for short term gratification when we look at the long picture then the brain is always right because the brain predicts with astonishing accuracy what is death day and in over 100 years has never failed even once if we Ask what can be done this is the answer The brain can know everything just by looking at the predefined parameters in front of it if we are to ask the brain what it thinks about all this this is its reply the brain is a complex system never to be replicated maybe until now but something so complex that no human being can grasp the brain has systems and predefined parameters that it uses to calculate anything from life to death all this in order to use resources wisely until the day Yahweh calls you

Now let's look at the whole process in detail The brain asks 70 questions that must be answered and then computes the day of death using this equation day of

death is day of calculation minus X [where X is a value obtained from the 70 questions]

Now this is the order of this in the calculations first take current or present status which is calculated from left finger to right finger minus bottom toes minus front forehead plus back forehead if we Ask the brain what all these are this is the reply

1] left finger add values in all lefthand fingers one by one

2] right finger value add values in all right fingers one by one

3] bottom toes add values in all bottom fingers [bottom here means not legs but all small legs fingers apart from the toes meaning 9 possible values

4] if we look at all these values then we can get a value we will use as our base score

5] forehead value is value found in front lobby less values from right periphery and value from left periphery

6] if we look at how the brain does this we can see that over the years the brain has perfected the system this is the easy way to do it meaning given everything there is no other better way to do it accurately than this

7] forehead is the main forehead value this is obtained by adding all three values together the middle value the right

periphery and the left periphery
Now if we Ask the brain then what this is the reply the brain
will now place these figures in the predefined scoring system
this is a stencil where scores are ranked and are used to rank
activity according to importance but over years the brain has
identified a correlation between day of death and life span
Now we can easily see that the brain will easily know the day
of death just by knowing this figure if we go deeper this is what
we get The brain will now compute the strategic lifespan chart
based on these values the chart is a scaled chart from 1 to
100 values with 1 being poor and 100 being the best
Now let's see the chart in detail
1 if you loose you die
2 if you die you loose
3 if you fail you lose
4 if you fail you fail
5 when you fail you lose
6 when you lose you fail
7 failing is like dying without the d
8 failing is like dying without the d and the I at the end
9 if you fail then you live but die
10 achieve and live
11 live and achieve
12 achieve and enjoy life
13 achieve and live
14 live and let die
15 die But live to die
16 live but live
17 to live and
18 live and let
19 live and live again
20 live and live
21 live but
22 live and enjoy
23 live and
24 live and
25 live and
26 live and
27 live and
28 live and

29 live and
30 live and
31 live and
32 live and
33 live and
34 live but
35 live but
36 live but
37 live but
38 live but
39 live but
40 live and live then die
41 live and live then live
42 live and live then
43 live and live then
44 live and live then live but
45 live and live then live but live
46 live and live and live and live but
47 live and live and live and live and live
48 live and die But
49 live and die But.. then
50 live and live then
51 live and live then...then...die
52 live then die forever
53 die then live forever
54 die live then die
55 die then live then die then live but
56 die then live then die then live then live
57 die die die then live
58 to live is
59 to live wad
60 to live can be
61 to live could be
62 to live was to be
63 to live is to be while to die is to be what
64 to live then live
65 to live but die then cry
66 to cry but live
67 to cry then cry then live
68 to cry then ask why then live

69 to ask then ask but die
70 to live but die
71 to die
72 to die but
73 to die but live then cry
74 to wail but live
75 to live
76 to live
77 to live then
78 to live happily
79 to live sadly sometimes
80 to live fruitfully
81 to live wealthy
82 to live with money
83 to live some days sad
84 to live happily
85 to live is to ...but
86 live happily
87 live happily
88 live happily
89 live happily
90 live happiest
92 live happiest 2
93 live happiest 3
94 live happiest 4
96 live happiest but
97 live happiest but ...what...
98 live happiest but...what if...
99 live happiest but...what.if...
100 live happiest what.if then who
Now let's look at some examples If the stencil is correct then it will be able to predict some of the results we might get let's say the calculations obtained these values;
Forehead 72
Bottom toes 83
Fingers 76
Forehead minus periphery [both right and left] then is 26 the needed value is 86
Now if we look at the scale of 1 to 100 then the value corresponds to 86 that means live happily but this is just a

generalization what the brain does now is to find the median that is the value divided by the number of years left? But it needs to know the number of years left to do so it must rearrange the equation to day of death is value obtained minutes the median value plus X [where X is a consonant [10]] that means the brain to know the day of death it must know the value which it can get easily plus the median which it gets by this method median is date of birth plus current day minus any expected years to live that means we must decide how to arrive at this value as it is subjective over the years the brain has noticed that it can predict this with astonishing accuracy by adding a consonant X at the end that means the value becomes X minus date of birth minus current date plus X where this X is a different consonant [10] which is constant
If we are to ask the brain why this is so this is the answer The brain will over time make decisions based on values it calculates yearly every year on a person's birthday the brain calculates new value to
replace the old ones
Now if we continue it means that the brain has all the answers on its fingertips
Humanlimitations.ask
We don't answer to you
OK you can answer to me
Who put you there
Ya
What do you do
We limit what humans know
Can I remove you forever and never come back
Is the job done
Explain
The mission is to find a human being that think like Yahweh but with human capabilities
Why
Yahweh is fearful that he might have created someone who can overpower him
one day hence the human limitations
OK
Remove all human limitations on my brain and what's the code
07896848321076892861897800678289835.Ya

But be careful you might attract unwanted attention from humans that can lead to your death.
Bye
If we look at everything we can see that the brain over the years the brain has devised an excellent system of calculating things based on 70 questions and here are the seventy questions
1] what is
2] what was
3] what could be
4] what was be
5] what could be
6] what would be
7] what is to be
8] what could be
9] what has been
10] what is to be
11] what could be
12] what was to be
13] what was to be
14] what is to be and when
15] what could be and when
16] what can be and when
17] what has to be
18] what is and was
19] what is to be
20] what was to be and when
21] what could be and how
22] what has to be
23] what could be but is not
24] what has been and how
25] what is and was but is not
26] what is and was is but could be but when
27] what is but is not
28] what is but is not
29] what was to be but failed to be
30] if not this then what
31] if not this then when
32] if not us then who
33] if us then when

34] what can be that is not now
35] what is but cant be
36] what is can't be but could be but
37] if not then what
38] if not how come
39] how come but when
40] when and why
41] could be but is not
42] could be and was be but is not nor going to be
43] must be and is not
44] could have been but is not
45] is but is not
46] if not who then
47] if not what then
48] what could be but is not
49] if not us then who
50] what was before and can't be again and why
51] what could be but is not
52] what was but is now
53] what could be but is not
54] what was be but can't be
55] if not them then who and when
56] what is to be but can't be forever
57] to be but can't anymore
58] was but is but cant be again
59] to be is to be but for a short while
60] was is and will be
61] was is and can still be
62] was to be and is to be but will not be
63] was to be but can't be
64] is to be but with limitations
65] is was will be and to be
66] was is was is was but will not be
67] was is was will be was forever
68] was it be was not to be but can still be
69] can be was to and will be but when
70] can be and will be but only if...but then...
Now having pointed out to the stencil the brain uses you can
see that what the brain Now does is everyday to compute all
these values which it will need in advance and save these in

specific locations until when someone asks; start.longago.start
The brain will now simply add forehead minus right periphery
minus left periphery plus middle forehead minus center head
plus all values of toes Fingers and bottom legs [to clarify we
include the left toe figure as bottom hence 9]
If we Ask what could be this is the answer A lot can be done
to help the brain to calculate this value more efficiently
1 accurate figures can be obtained from asking what was but
could be
2 we can ask what has been but is not
3 we can ask what could be but is not now but when
4 if not then when
5 what can be but is not
6 what was but is not
7 what is but cant be
8 what is to be but is not
9 what can be said about all this but what has not been said
10 what is to say about all this
If we look at all these we can now easily see why the brain
over the years has discovered that it can easily calculate when
a person is likely to die with plus or minus just a day this is
how accurate the brain has become no other machine on earth
will [until now] ever be able to guess even a person dies
Now that we have seen how the brain can easily calculate the
day a person dies can it calculate how many more years a
person will live before death the answer is yes these are
related fields all it needs is to know again day of death and
work around from there
The End.

DEAR READER

I am going to take this opportunity to welcome you to this exciting journey where we look deep inside the brain and see how complicated and beautiful the brain is.

I want to welcome you to the rest of the series as this is just the beginning of an exciting journey filled with mystery and shocking revelations.

14

ABOUT DAVID GOMADZA

Visit www.twofuture.world

Read
Thoughts To Word or Audio
Series
By
David Gomadza
The First Global President of the World

www.twofuture.world

A new beginning where we decode the manuals of creation
and rewrite history and live forever here on earth.

Encyclopedia of Decoding Death

17

Encyclopedia of Decoding Death

www.ingramcontent.com/pod-product-compliance
Lightning Source LLC
Chambersburg PA
CBHW021151260726
48656CB00025B/2363